STEP-UP
SCIENCE

Friction

Louise and Richard Spilsbury

Evans

Published by Evans Brothers Limited
2A Portman Mansions
Chiltern Street
London W1U 6NR

© Evans Brothers Limited 2007

Produced for Evans Brothers Limited by
White-Thomson Publishing Ltd,
Bridgewater Business Centre,
210 High Street,
Lewes, East Sussex BN7 2NH

Printed in China by New Era Printing Co. Ltd

Project manager: Rachel Minay

Designer: Flick, Book Design and Graphics

Consultant: Jackie Holderness,
Educational Consultant and Writer

The rights of Louise and Richard Spilsbury to be
identified as the authors of this work has been
asserted by the authors in accordance with the
Copyright, Designs and Patents Act 1988.

British Library Cataloguing in Publication Data

Friction. – (Step-up science)

1. Friction – Juvenile literature
531.1'134

ISBN-13: 9780237532116
ISBN-10: 0237532115

Acknowledgements:

The authors would like to thank Scott Fisher,
teacher at Stokenham Area Primary School for his
invaluable comments and advice on this series.

Picture acknowledgements:

Martyn f. Chillmaid: front cover tl, 12, 13l, 13r,
16b. CORBIS: front cover tr (Pete Saloutos), pages
4 (Duomo), 11t (Larry Williams/zefa), 26 (Pete
Saloutos), 27b (Valdrin Xhemaj/epa). Getty images:
page 9t. Istockphoto: front cover (main), title page,
pages 5t, 5b, 6, 7r, 7bl, 9b, 10, 14, 15t, 17, 18t,
18b, 19l, 19r, 20, 22r, 23r, 24, 25t, 25b. OSF/
Photolibrary: pages 8 (Karl E Deckart/Phototake
Inc), 11b (Rogers Martin), 16t (Mode Images Ltd),
21r (James Watt), 22l (Bill Bachmann), 23l (Paul
Franklin). Science Photo Library: page 21l (Takeshi
Takahara). Speedo International Limited, 2006:
page 27t.

Illustrations by Hattie Spilsbury (page 7tl) and Ian
Thompson (page 15b).

Contents

Forces

Things move in many different ways. Some move from place to place, others might twist, slide or turn on one spot. Nothing moves by itself. Things move because of forces, which are pushes or pulls.

Moving forces

A door moves when we push or pull it, and a car moves because an engine pushes the wheels around. Other forces push or pull, too. Drop a ball and it falls to the ground because the force of gravity pulls it towards the Earth. Iron filings move towards a magnet because the force of magnetism pulls them.

Two by two

Forces act in pairs. Any object can have a force or be acted upon by another force. If one force is stronger than the other, the stronger force will make the weaker force or object move away from the direction of the stronger force.

If two forces are equal then the object stays still. For example, if something is hanging on an elastic band gravity pulls it down, stretching the elastic band. However, the pulling force of the band also works in the opposite direction, so the object stays still. The two forces are balanced.

▲ When you throw a ball in the air, the force of your throw is — for a short time — greater than that of gravity.

Gravity cartoon

Draw a cartoon or diagram to explain the idea of gravity to younger children.

Friction

If we try to gently push a book across a table, we can feel another force. This force seems to be resisting our force or even pushing back. The force is called friction. There is friction between any two objects or surfaces that touch. This force always acts in the opposite direction to an object's motion. When we push the book harder, our force gets stronger than friction so the book moves.

Slowing up

Friction is a force that opposes motion, so it slows moving things down. It may sometimes seem like a nuisance, because it means we have to work harder to walk or cycle a bike. For example, the wheels of a bicycle will only turn when the force of the cyclist's pedalling is greater than the friction between the tyres and the road surface.

▲ A rollercoaster is powered at the beginning of a ride, when the train is pulled up the first hill. Then its own weight and gravity keep it moving. Because rollercoaster designers know that friction will ultimately slow the train down, they make each hill lower than the last so that the rollercoaster can make it over each one.

◀ In order to move, vehicles burn fuel in their engines. A lorry uses more fuel than a car to travel the same distance. How does friction and the lorry's greater size help explain this?

Useful friction

Friction makes it harder to move things, so we can use it to help control movement. Without friction, many of the things we do every day, such as walking, writing and eating, would be very difficult or even impossible.

Getting a grip

Friction is happening all around us. People can cross their legs, when sitting, because friction stops their legs slipping apart. Shoelaces stay tied up because of friction between different parts of the lace. And without friction, a person couldn't grip a glass of juice or a spoon to have breakfast!

The next step

Walking relies on friction. In the first part of a step, a person places the sole of one foot on the ground and pushes back against it. The friction or grip between the sole and the ground stops the foot slipping backwards. The person can then shift their body forward and use the other leg to take the next step. It is also friction that helps the person to stop, when they push their feet against the ground to slow down and stop forward movement.

▲ *Without friction, it would be very hard to walk anywhere, but especially down slopes. We would slip and slide around, as if we were wearing socks on ice.*

Paul Klee

This picture was inspired by the Swiss artist Paul Klee (1879–1940) who said he liked to take lines for a walk when he drew.

Take a line for a walk yourself. What happens when you press the pencil harder? What happens when you don't press down the pencil?

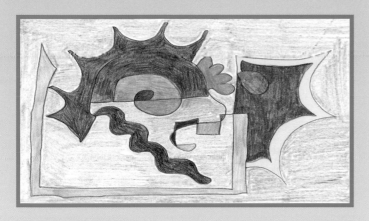

▶ *Thanks to friction, the wheels of a train can grip the railway tracks and travel safely.*

Drive on

Friction makes cars safer to use. Friction between the tyres and the road stops a vehicle from slipping and sliding when it moves or changes direction. Brakes slow a car down using friction. When the driver pushes down the brake pedal, motors press brake pads against the moving wheels, slowing them down. Have you ever heard a car screeching when braking? This happens because the wheels have stopped spinning but the car is still sliding along the road. The noise you hear is caused by friction.

▼ *Pencils write because of friction. Friction between the graphite (pencil lead) and paper rubs off a layer of graphite to leave a mark.*

Reducing friction

Investigate ways of reducing friction. Get an old tray and some small toy cars, and experiment with ways of making the surface of the tray slippery. Making surfaces slippery reduces friction. What happens to the toy cars when you push them over a slippery surface?

Friction factors

Friction is sometimes described as a contact force. The amount of contact, and therefore friction, depends on the size and weight of an object and what it is moving over. The type of surface an object moves over will affect how much friction there is.

Surface textures

Friction occurs mostly because bumps on surfaces tend to catch on one another as they slide past each other. So the rougher the surface something moves against, the greater the friction. That is why there is more friction between two rough surfaces, like two sheets of sandpaper, than between a rough and a smooth surface, such as sandpaper and wood. However, there is still friction even between two apparently smooth surfaces. Even smooth surfaces have many tiny ridges and grooves, although we cannot see them.

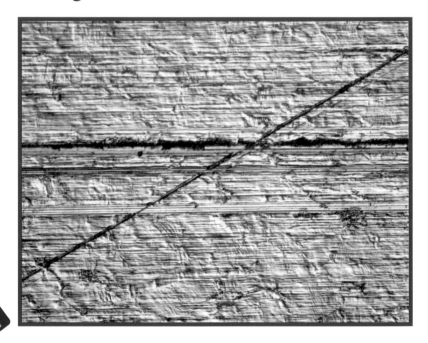

▲ Looking through a microscope at smooth surfaces like metal, you see many tiny bumps and grooves. These ridges can get stuck in the grooves of other surfaces, causing friction. This **magnified** picture shows the surface of brushed steel.

Friction investigation

How do you think the amount of friction will differ when you pull a wooden block over four different surfaces: a large sheet of sandpaper, a wooden floor, a plastic bench top and a carpet? Explain why you should use the same wooden block each time. How will you record your results? Was your prediction correct?

Weight

Another factor is weight. Heavier objects create more friction than lighter objects because they press surfaces together with more force. That is why a brick would be harder to push across the floor than a block of wood of the same size.

Surface area

Surface area is the total area of the outside of a shape or object. The amount of friction between two objects depends on the size of the surface areas that make contact. So, for example, a wide, flat object like a book would create more friction when pushed across the floor face down than it would if pushed on its side or spine.

▲ *Imagine pushing a go-kart along first with a small child and then with a large adult sitting on it. Which passenger would cause the greatest friction?*

Carts and barrows

The invention of carts and barrows – around 5,000 years ago – made people's lives much easier. A heavy object is much easier to push in a wheelbarrow than across the ground.

Dragging a heavy object across the ground causes friction between the whole area of the object and the ground. In a wheelbarrow, the object's weight only causes friction between the ground and a small area of the wheel.

Moving on different surfaces

Surfaces that create a lot of friction when objects move over them, such as roads, are called high-friction surfaces. Low-friction surfaces, such as ice, do not provide grip and so moving objects slide over them.

Safer surfaces

High-friction surfaces include carpets, rugs, grass and soil. These surfaces are safe to walk and run across and carry things over without slipping. Roads throughout the world are made from tarmac, a high-friction surface. Tarmac is a mixture of gravel and tar. Tarmac provides enough friction to stop vehicles slipping when they turn corners or brake. But it is also smooth enough for vehicles to travel freely.

Slipping and sliding

Some surfaces get more slippery when they become wet. People are more likely to slip on a wet floor or on wet grass, because there is less friction between the soles of their shoes and the thin layer of water on the ground. A moving vehicle on a wet road takes much longer to stop when it brakes suddenly because water reduces the contact between car tyres and the tarmac.

◀ A runway has a high-friction surface. This gives good grip to planes as they pick up speed for take-off, and helps them slow down when they land.

Smooth low-friction runners on the bottom of ice skates or sledges mean you can move quickly across a low-friction surface such as ice.

Low-friction fun

Moving on some low-friction surfaces can be fun. Playground and water slides have very smooth, low-friction surfaces so we can slide down them quickly. Ice is a very low-friction surface. That is why people slip and slide across it so easily when they go sledging or ice skating. Sledges usually have plastic or steel surfaces on the runners. These materials have smooth surfaces that will slide easily over ice and snow.

◀ *Ice is a low-friction surface so penguins, who are not fast walkers, can speed along by sliding along on their tummies. They wouldn't get very far if they tried this on grass!*

Friction lists

Make a list of high-friction and a list of low-friction surfaces. Which of your lists is longer?

Measuring forces

Forces such as friction are measured with an instrument called a forcemeter. A forcemeter measures force in units called newtons (which we sometimes write as 'N'). Different forcemeters measure different amounts of newtons.

Sir Isaac Newton

Sir Isaac Newton was the scientist who first explored the effects of gravity. He saw that apples fell downwards from trees and worked out that there must be a force pulling them down. The unit of force is named after Newton. The Earth pulls on a mass of 100 g (the size of a medium-sized apple) with a force of 1 newton.

How do forcemeters work?

Hold an elastic band in one hand or hook it over something and pull the other end. If you pull hard and use enough force, you will stretch the band. If you tie different objects to the end of the band you will see that the heaviest objects produce the biggest force and stretch the band furthest. This is how a forcemeter works. The pulling force of an object stretches a spring inside the forcemeter. The bigger the force, the more the spring stretches and the higher the reading on the forcemeter.

▲ This forcemeter has a scale that goes up to 10 newtons. It is useful for measuring weaker forces. Some forcemeters go up to 20 or 50 newtons and are able to measure stronger forces.

Make a forcemeter

Find instructions to make your own forcemeter at http://quest. nasa.gov/projects/jason/documents/ Friction%20Project-Martin% 20Family.doc

▲ *If you pull a trainer and a slipper across a floor, the trainer will give a higher reading on a forcemeter because it has the best grip and so provides the most friction.*

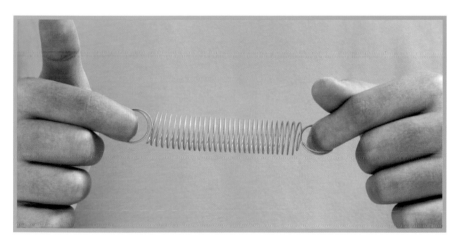

◄ *Springs are used to measure the size of a force because they are elastic. They can be stretched by a force, but when the force is taken away they return to their original size and shape.*

Friction and weight

What do you think will happen to the amount of friction between a shoe and the floor when we add weights to the shoe to make it heavier? Plan an investigation using one flat shoe, a set of different weights, a surface such as a wooden or linoleum floor and a forcemeter. Put a weight in the shoe and pull the shoe across a distance of 2 metres. Repeat for each weight. Record the measurements you get on the forcemeter each time.

Why must you do this test using only one shoe and one surface? What else do you need to do to make the test fair? Plan how to record the results.

Reducing friction

Reducing friction in machines is vital because friction can cause problems. For one thing, friction makes things hotter. In machines, kinetic energy changes into heat. This not only wastes energy but it can also damage machine parts. Another problem with friction is that, when moving parts of machines rub against each other, they can wear away. Friction between parts can also make unwanted noise.

How lubrication helps

One way to reduce friction is by lubrication (or making the surfaces more slippery). If oil is added to the parts of a machine, instead of rubbing against each other, they slide on the layer of oil. Oil on moving parts in car engines or factory machines reduces heat and stops the parts wearing each other away. The parts will also move more easily and work more efficiently.

Lubrication can also solve the problem of noise that friction can cause. For example, if the hinge of a door squeaks when it rubs against the door frame, some drops of oil will reduce the friction and stop the noise.

▼ *This mechanic is checking the oil in a car engine. Without oil, friction created by engine parts rubbing together would cause them to become too hot. This could make the engine overheat and even catch fire.*

These **abseilers** are wearing gloves. This increases the grip between their hands and the rope, but also stops friction burns when the rope pulls quickly across their hands when they are abseiling.

Ball bearings

People also use ball bearings to reduce friction in machines. These are smooth metal balls, usually made of steel, which can roll smoothly. In a machine, two solid surfaces sliding over each other create a lot of friction. When a solid surface slides over a surface made up of ball bearings, it rolls quickly because there is much less friction. Ball bearings are also used to reduce friction in bicycle parts, skateboards and rollerblades.

How ball bearings work

Find out how ball bearings work by doing this investigation with marbles. Get a lid that fits over the bottom of an old soup tin. Put a blob of plasticine on both ends of a pencil and one in the middle to stick the pencil to the top of the lid. Try spinning the lid. Now put marbles on the soup can under the lid and spin the lid again.

The marbles act like ball bearings and help the lid spin smoothly.

Pencil   Plasticine

Marbles

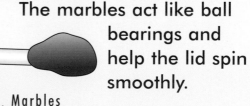

Increasing friction

There are many reasons why we increase friction. Sometimes we need to slow or control movement on low-friction surfaces to make things safer. For example, on rainy days, smooth tyres on racing cars are changed to tyres with better grip. Sometimes, things simply work better with an improved grip.

Extra bumps, grooves and ridges

Adding bumps and grooves to a surface increases its surface area, and so increases friction. That is why people add materials with bumpy surfaces to steps that might get slippery, for example on buses. Tennis rackets and bicycle handlebars have ridged handles so that we can grip them well even when our hands are damp and sweaty.

▲ Racing cars often have to make **pit stops** like this to have new tyres put on. A racing car's softer tyres provide more grip, but they also wear out fast.

▶ One of these shoes will slip and slide easily. The other will create more friction with the ground and be good for gripping. Which is which?

Burning rubber

Normal car tyres have treads to improve their hold on the road. These are grooved shapes moulded into the rubber. Tyres with deeper, wider treads will increase friction on ice or snow. So they can go faster, racing car tyres have less tread and their tyres are made of soft sticky rubber. The friction between the road and tyres makes them get hotter, and the rubber gets stickier and grips better. Some tyres get so hot that they blow out or burst!

Scientific skateboards

Discover the link between skateboards and science at http://www.exploratorium.edu/skateboarding/

Research how skateboarders use grip tape to get the friction they need to drag a board into the air. Then write up an explanation in your own words.

Sticky situations

Sticky powders or substances can also increase friction and help us grip things. Gymnasts put sticky powder on their hands to improve their hold on the bars. Violinists put rosin on their bows to increase the friction between the bow and the strings to make the strings vibrate and create sounds and notes. Surfers put wax on the top of their surfboards to stop them sliding off when they ride a wave.

The surface of this surfboard has wax on the middle of it. This increases the friction between the surfer's feet and the board and provides a better grip.

Air resistance

Friction does not only exist between two solid objects, like your feet and the ground. It can also exist between a solid, like a parachute, and a gas, such as air. Air resistance is a kind of friction that slows down objects that are moving through the air.

Friction with the air

Friction with air is harder to understand than friction with another solid because we cannot see air. But we can feel it! We can feel air pushing against us when we walk in the wind.

Air is a substance that has weight like any other substance. It can rub on the surface of a moving object causing friction. Air resistance is also sometimes called drag. It 'drags' on things and slows them down.

▲ Dandelion plants have parachute-like hairs on their seeds. These increase air resistance and help the seeds float to new places to grow.

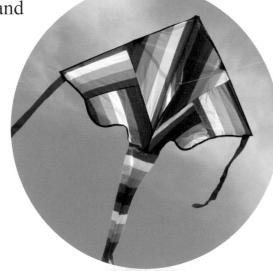

▶ You can feel air resistance if you pull on kite strings on a windy day.

Paper aeroplanes

Make your own paper aeroplanes to see which shapes move better through the air. For ideas go to http://phoenix.gov/AVIATION/kids/airplanes.html

You could try making your planes out of different kinds of paper, to see which works best.

Flying forwards

Air resistance slows down aeroplanes in the air, just as it slows down cars on the ground. The faster something moves, the greater the effects of air resistance on it. To fly at high speeds through the sky, the thrusting force of an aeroplane's engine must be greater than the air resistance. Over the course of a ten-hour flight, a Boeing 747 plane burns up to 150,000 litres of fuel. An average car uses 1,400 litres of fuel per year.

Out in space

In space there is no air, so there is no air resistance to slow things down. Once spacecraft leave Earth's atmosphere and reach space, they can turn their engines off and still keep moving! They travel away from Earth in a straight line and only have to use their engines when they want to change direction.

▲ A jet engine burns a lot of fuel to make the force of its movement forwards greater than air resistance and make a plane fly fast.

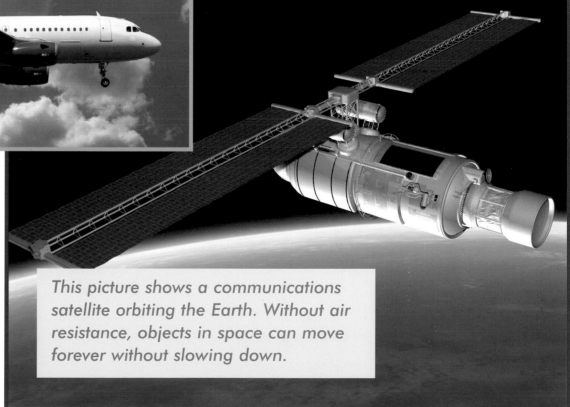

This picture shows a communications satellite orbiting the Earth. Without air resistance, objects in space can move forever without slowing down.

Investigating air resistance

Air resistance can be a useful force for slowing things down. A parachute would not work without it. When a parachutist jumps from a plane, gravity pulls him or her down, but when the air fills the parachute, air resistance slows the fall. The force of gravity is still stronger than the air resistance, so the parachute drops, but slowly enough to be safe.

Parachute investigation

Investigate whether the size of a parachute affects how long it takes to fall. Cut squares from an old sheet to make three parachutes of different sizes: 10 cm x 10 cm, 20 cm x 20 cm and 30 cm x 30 cm. For each parachute, attach thread to each corner with a safety pin. Tie the other ends of the thread to a clothes peg (the parachutist). Why is it important that you make the parachutes from the same fabric and with the same shape and design? Using a watch with a second hand, or a stopwatch, time how long it takes each parachute to fall. Record your results and explain what they show you.

SAFETY: Do this investigation with an adult. Be very careful about leaning over stairwells or standing on tables.

▲ *This sports parachute has a rectangular* canopy*. As the parachutist falls, air is trapped in pockets in the canopy. The air pockets form a curved shape that helps lift the parachutist so that he or she can stay in the air longer. Parachutists change direction by pulling on the cords that attach them to the canopy.*

Surface area

The greater the surface area of an object, the greater its air resistance. Sailors reduce the area of their sails when it is very windy to catch less wind and stop their boat from being pulled along too quickly. To catch more wind, they open out the sails to their full extent.

You can investigate this with a sheet of paper. What can you do to make it fall more quickly or more slowly? Try dropping it flat first, then screwed up in a ball, or folded up small. How does changing its surface area affect its air resistance?

The flaps of skin around its arms and legs increase the surface area of a flying squirrel's body. How does this help it to parachute from tree to tree?

▲ *Car designers want to reduce air resistance so that a vehicle can travel fast but not waste fuel. New cars are designed so that air flows easily over them and they are tested out in a wind tunnel like this.*

Aerodynamic aeroplanes

Aeroplanes, like arrows and rockets, are designed to be aerodynamic. They have smoother, more streamlined shapes to cut down on air resistance so they can slip smoothly through the air.

Aeroplanes are also designed to tuck in their wheels during flight. This helps to keep a smooth outline and further reduce air resistance.

Water resistance

Why is it hard to wade or swim through water at the seaside or swimming pool? The force that is slowing us down is a kind of friction called water resistance. We feel the effects of friction more strongly in water than in air, because water is denser than air.

▲ *Swimming is a good form of exercise because you have to work hard to move against the resistance of water, which is ten times stronger than air resistance.*

Going down

Friction always acts in the opposite direction to the direction an object is moving, so when an object is dropped into water the resistance of water works against the object and slows it down. We can feel the force of water pushing up if we try to push a rubber ring or float underwater. When an object floats, it is because the water is pushing up on the object. Upthrust is the force that pushes things up. On land, solid objects like chairs give us upthrust. In water, we and other things float because of upthrust. Upthrust in water is also called buoyancy.

▼ *We can use arrows to show the direction and relative size of forces. Gravity is pulling the rubber duck down and upthrust is pushing the duck up. The forces are balanced so the duck floats.*

gravity

upthrust

Boats and water resistance

Thrust provided by the wind in a sailboat or the engines in a motor vessel is the force that moves a boat forwards. Water resistance is the backward force that slows the boat down. Since water is dense, moving through it takes a lot of energy. In a boat, this means using a lot of energy or fuel.

Underwater animals

Submarines use engines and propellers to thrust forwards underwater, but aquatic animals have a variety of ways to overcome water resistance and move around. A fish moves through water by waving its body and tail back and forth. Whales and dolphins use their tails to push against the water and move.

▼ *Frogs have powerful legs and webbed feet, which they use to push against the water.*

Make a hovercraft

Hovercrafts are special boats that float on a cushion of air just above the water. Air resistance is much less than the dragging effect of water resistance so this enables hovercrafts to go faster. Make your own hovercraft using an unwanted CD, a balloon and a cotton reel. See the Planet Science website http://www.planet-science.com for instructions.

Reducing water resistance

To save fuel and energy, boat designers look carefully at ways of reducing water resistance. The two main factors that can alter water resistance are weight and shape.

Lightweight boats

Boat designers use materials such as fibreglass and carbon fibre to make speedboats because these are light materials. Light, small boats sit high in the water, so there is less water for them to have to push against.

Some of the fastest motorboats have hydrofoils. These are small wings that are positioned under the water. They lift the front end of the hull (body) of the boat above the water and thus reduce water resistance.

Streamlined shapes

A boat's shape has an impact on its ability to move in water and the speed at which it can go. Just as vehicles that move through the air have streamlined shapes to reduce air resistance, boats have pointed front ends to reduce friction in the water. A long, narrow, streamlined shape allows the water to flow past easily and smoothly. Streamlined boats help to save money by using less fuel because there is less water resistance.

◄ Boats move faster if they are light, have powerful engines to overcome water resistance and have a pointed bow (or front) and a streamlined hull to cut through the water.

▲ *Dolphins spend their lives moving fast through water to catch fish to eat. Can you think of three more marine, or water, animals with streamlined body shapes?*

▼ *Manatees graze slowly on underwater plants. Their bodies are not streamlined. How does a manatee's body shape reflect and suit its lifestyle?*

Water resistance test

Plan an investigation to test different shapes for water resistance. Cut the top part off a large empty plastic drinks bottle and fill it with water. Then take four equal-sized pieces of plasticine and make them into four small different shapes: a ball, a flat shape such as a square or disc (like a small frisbee), a cube and a torpedo shape. Which shape do you think will have the highest water resistance and take longest to fall through the water? How will you time the test and make it fair? Record your results in a bar chart.

Sports round-up

What makes a winner in sport? Is it skill, dedication or training, or is it an athlete's understanding of how to reduce or increase friction, water and air resistance to improve his or her performance?

Aerodynamic shapes and cycling

Aerodynamic shapes are those that reduce air resistance. Think about how racing cyclists use aerodynamics to get ahead. How does the shape of the cycle helmet reduce air resistance? And why do racing bikes have low handlebars?

The right shoes

There are a great variety of shoe soles for different sports and it is vital to have the right sort of sole to get the right amount of friction. Can you explain why football boots have studs to grip the pitch? Why do ice skaters have shoes that make them balance on a blade? And why do gymnasts need shoes with soles that are completely flexible to bend with the feet, and with smooth yet high-friction surfaces? Can you think of other examples of sports shoe styles?

▲ This racing cyclist is reducing air resistance in a number of ways. How does the raised seat put her in a more aerodynamic position?

Body suits

Swimmers could expend more than 90 per cent of their energy just trying to overcome water resistance, leaving only 10 per cent of their energy for speed. So the more they can reduce water resistance, the faster they can swim. Some swimmers reduce water resistance by shaving all the hair off their bodies. Swimsuits are usually skin-tight so they do not absorb water, which would make the swimmer heavier. Some swimsuits even have tiny grooves along the back to reduce the amount of water a swimmer carries on his or her back.

▼ *This Olympic swimmer is wearing a special swimming costume that is water-repellent, so it does not absorb water. The costume is also designed to channel water away from the body to reduce water resistance.*

◄ *In curling competitions, curlers brush the ice in front of the puck to make the surface even smoother. This reduces friction and allows the puck to travel further.*

Sports report

Imagine you are a sports reporter. Write a newspaper or magazine report about the role that friction plays in a sport that you like or know a lot about.

Glossary

abseiler — someone who descends from a high place such as a rockface by sliding down a rope.

aerodynamic — used to describe a shape that reduces air resistance.

aerodynamics — the science behind ways to reduce air resistance.

air resistance — the friction between air and an object moving through it.

ball bearings — smooth metal balls used in machines to reduce friction between moving parts.

buoyancy — the upward force on an object in water. Buoyancy is what allows things to float.

canopy — the part of a parachute that fills with air and which is often shaped like an umbrella when in use.

dense — used to describe how thick or concentrated a substance is.

drag — another word for air and water resistance.

force — a push or a pull. Magnetism and gravity are examples of forces.

forcemeter — an instrument used to measure force in newtons (N). Forcemeters are sometimes called newtonmeters.

friction — the force that resists motion between two objects that rub against each other.

gravity — the force that pulls everything down towards the centre of the Earth. Gravity is why we stay on the surface instead of floating into space.

high friction — used to describe a surface that creates a lot of friction, for example a rough surface like grass.

hull — the frame or body of a boat or ship.

kinetic energy — kinetic energy is movement energy.

low friction — used to describe a surface that creates little friction, for example a smooth surface like ice.

lubrication — a way of using oil or another kind of slippery substance to reduce friction between moving objects.

magnetism   the force that certain metals have that pulls other metal objects towards them.

magnified   enlarged by being viewed through special magnifying lenses.

newton   the unit used for measuring forces.

pit stop   the pit is an area by a racing track where racing drivers stop during a race. During a pit stop, the car can be quickly refuelled or serviced or have its tyres changed.

rosin   a natural substance from pine trees that is heated and hardened into blocks.

spring   a coiled metal wire that returns to its original shape after it has been pulled and stretched.

streamlined   used to describe something that has a smooth, sleek shape that reduces water or air resistance.

surface area   the total area of the outside of a shape or object.

tar   a thick, black, oily, natural material, which is made in the same way as fossil fuels, such as petrol or coal, from the bodies of decayed plants and animals.

torpedo   a torpedo-shaped object is a tube or cylinder shape and usually has a pointed head and a slightly bulging middle.

tread   the pattern of grooves that is moulded into tyre rubber.

upthrust   the upward force on an object in water.

vibrate   to move or jiggle about on the spot.

water resistance   the friction between water and an object moving through it.

wind tunnel   a tube-like room where wind is blown by a large fan towards a vehicle to test how air flows over it.

For teachers and parents

This book is designed to support and extend the learning objectives for Unit 4E of the QCA Science Schemes of Work.

The children will have already worked on forces and this book builds on that knowledge. Friction, air and water resistance are forces with many everyday contexts that are interesting for children to read about and many of which they can experience first-hand.

Throughout this book and throughout their own investigative work, children should be aware that science is based on evidence and they should have the opportunity to:

- Turn questions into an investigation.
- Predict results.
- Understand the need to collect sufficient evidence.
- Understand the need to conduct a fair test.
- Choose and use appropriate measuring or investigation equipment.
- Record results using tables and bar charts, sometimes using ICT.
- Interpret evidence by making observations, comparisons and conclusions using scientific language.

There are opportunities for cross-curricular work in literacy, numeracy, history, art, design technology and ICT.

SUGGESTED FURTHER ACTIVITIES

Pages 4 - 5 Forces
Children could draw examples of four pushes and four pulls.

Children can have fun learning about forces, including gravity and friction, at the interactive website http://www.bbc.co.uk/schools/revisewise/science/physical/12b_act.shtml and at http://www.bbc.co.uk/schools/scienceclips/ages/8_9/friction.shtml. At http://www.ngfl-cymru.org.uk/vtc/Phase2delivery/Wales/WalesSynd%5F20030219/Science/Keystage2/Physicalprocess/Forcescardowner/Introduction/default.htm you can download a lesson on how gravity and friction affect a car moving down a ramp.

Children can design a fairground ride at http://www.bbc.co.uk/schools/digger/teachers/7_9_how_to_use_science.shtml. They can add labelled arrows showing the effects of the different forces at play.

Pages 6 - 7 Useful friction
Children can see some pictures by Paul Klee and find out more about the artist at http://www.tumbletales.com/masters/Gallery/Klee/gklee.html#%20. This could be linked to Art and Design Unit 4C, Journeys, with children taking a pencil for a walk to illustrate their journey from school to home.

Children could write and illustrate a story that describes how friction is useful to them or to a character in a story.

Children could make an illustrated poster showing everyday activities where friction plays a role. They could draw examples themselves, download pictures from the Internet or cut pictures from magazines.

In PE sessions, focus children's attention on the way friction helps them in the activities they do, from running to rounders.

Pages 8 - 9 Friction factors
Children could design and make their own moving toys and then use them to test friction. For example, they should think about what found objects or materials will make wheels that will grip the 'road'?

Pages 10 - 11 Moving on different surfaces
Children could try the 'Scratch and Slide' activity at the 'Wondernet' site at http://www.chemistry.org/portal/a/c/s/1/wondernetdisplay.html?DOC=wondernet\activities\friction\scratch.html to test the effects of different surfaces on friction.

Pages 12 - 13 Measuring forces
Children could test and measure how high a ramp has to be before a brick will slide down it and make a bar chart to record results. Use database and graphing tools to produce a bar chart on the computer. See http://www.kented.org.uk/ngfl/subjects/science/Friction/friction4.html

Pages 14 - 15 Reducing friction

You can download a simple worksheet that helps children understand how friction creates heat and to see the effects of lubrication on friction using hand cream. Go to http://www.galaxy.net/%7ek12/machines/fr_over2.shtml

You could link friction to a human body topic. At joints such as knees and elbows we have smooth cartilage to reduce friction and our body produces a lubricant (synovial fluid) where bones meet. Children could label joints on a skeleton and think about why it is important to reduce friction at these points.

Pages 16 - 17 Increasing friction

Mr Zippy's trainers! At http://www.sycd.co.uk/primary/mr_zippy/index.htm# children answer a series of questions about what makes a fast, waterproof trainer. They can then design a trainer of their own by dragging and dropping different colours and styles.

Pages 18 - 19 Air resistance

Children can investigate wind resistance with the aid of an online simulation at http://puzzling.caret.cam.ac.uk/game.php?game=parachute

Children could link this work to history of transport and investigate the way vehicles have changed and how they have become more streamlined over the years as knowledge of forces and technology has advanced.

Children could investigate the heat shield on Apollo 10, which was made of heat resistant materials to withstand the friction heat on re-entry. See http://www.sln.org/pieces/cych/apollo%2010/teachers/resources/resources4.html

Pages 20 - 21 Investigating air resistance

At the web page http://www.rolls-royce.com/education/schools/resources/far_ans.pdf there are worksheets about forces and air resistance that show the children where to draw arrows to indicate the direction and size of forces on an object.

You can extend parachute-making work with activities at http://www.seed.slb.com/en/scictr/lab/parachute/notes.htm

Pages 22 - 23 Water resistance

During a PE swimming session you could get the children to think about water resistance and upthrust. For example, by trying to force a float or a buoyant ball under the water or finding out about how much easier it is to lift someone when in the water than on land.

Looking at how animals move in water could link to a project on habitats and animal movement. Animals move in different ways depending on the habitat in which they live. For example, snails overcome friction with the ground by moving across a slimy trail, which they secrete.

Pages 24 - 25 Reducing water resistance

Children could design and make a boat out of found or recycled materials or simply from plasticine. They could test and race boats, by simply pushing them from a starting point, to see which goes the fastest or furthest. They could then discuss and evaluate designs, thinking about which was the most streamlined and how different shapes affect upthrust and water resistance.

Work on boats and streamlined shapes could link to a Greek history project about triremes, ancient Greek warships. Children could learn how the boats were powered (by numerous rowers) and look at boat illustrations on ancient Greek pots.

Pages 26 - 27 Sports round-up

The class could discuss the forces at play in other sporting activities, such as air resistance in sailing, water resistance in canoeing, gravity in pole-vaulting and friction in relation to grip on sports equipment such as tennis racquets.

Index